YOUR RETIREMENT SHOULD BE MORE

YOUR
RETIREMENT
SHOULD BE
MORE

HOW TO HARNESS THE POWER OF **MORE** IN YOUR RETIREMENT

JOHN SHREWSBURY & JANET WALKER

Printed in the United States of America.
Library of Congress Control Number:
ISBN Paperback: 978-1-949639-25-4
ISBN eBook: 978-1-949639-26-1

Cover Design: Sean Shrewsbury
Layout Design: George Stevens
Illustrations: Casey Cochran

CONTENTS

ACKNOWLEDGMENTS

Long careers in the financial industry don't happen without the unwavering support of the families of the financial professionals. To our families, we thank you for the freedom to pursue our passion, to build our dreams, and to share them with you. The long hours, hard work, and time away have all been to provide for the needs, comfort, and dreams of each of you. We thank you for all you have given to make it possible.

To our spouses, in particular, Debbie Shrewsbury and Steven Walker, thank you for doing what we could not do. When we have been gone on business, you have each in your respective households fulfilled the roles of two parents. You have kept everything going that would have fallen apart without you: doctors' appointments, transportation to and from school, all the sporting events, horseback riding and band, home-cooked meals, and carryout when you couldn't cook. Without you, we would not have been able to survive, much less thrive. You are blessings to us!

Much gratitude is owed to our team at GenWealth Financial Advisors. You are not employees; you are members of our extended family whom we have chosen to share our lives and our business with. Each of you is valued for who you are and what you bring to our clients.

The catalyst of this book was born from a conversation with advisor Charlie Skinner as we discussed one of his prospective clients' limited view of retirement as being only about their investment account. Special thanks also go to Teresa Arrigo and Angela Crowe for their work in proofreading this book when our eyes were too tired, and our minds too crowded, to communicate clearly.

To our entire Leadership Team: Alisha Macom, Kimmy James, Sean Shrewsbury, Tim Key, and Mona Khairi: we could not do what we do without the passion and dedication you show every day. Thank you for leading with passion and purpose.

Much gratitude goes to Pastors Mark Evans and Doug Pruitt, who are always there to offer guidance and direction when the path isn't clear. You both have been instrumental in helping us and GenWealth fulfill our God-given purpose.

Speaking of purpose, a big thank you to our clients. You are the "why" of what we do. From the beginning, the mission statement of GenWealth has been:

To provide wise, knowledgeable counsel through trusted advisors in order for our clients to realize their God-given financial purpose in their lives and to assist them in leaving a legacy for generations to come.

This book is dedicated to you and is the next evolution in that process. We are dedicated to helping you harness the *Power of MORE!*

FOREWORD

BY BURT WHITE,

CHIEF INVESTMENT OFFICER, LPL FINANCIAL

Who doesn't want more?

The reality is that wanting more is a universal truth - something that has stood the test of time, been the storyline of infinite movies, fueled the dreams of millions of people and has been the subject line of too many prayers to count. MORE is the most sought-after destination on Earth.

But too many feel further from having MORE than ever before. What most miss is that MORE is not a destination; it is a journey. And like any journey, it requires a plan, time and movement. And in our world of immediacy, impatience and inwardness, too few stumble their way to actually getting to MORE. A world that has made everything so easy, so do-it-yourself, so turnkey – the tyranny of convenience has conditioned too many of us to expect that MORE is as easy as plugging in that new electronic device or a fast search on the internet.

Holding us back, however, is not our potential for MORE, it is our perception of what it is and what it takes to achieve it. Have you ever been singing along to a song on the radio and realized that tens of thousands of people are singing along with you? A perfect harmony all over the city that only God can hear. Or that 6am alarm that wakes you up simultaneous to millions of others around the world to the promise of a new day and a new opportunity. Our connectedness is greater than we can even imagine. This is the power of MORE. If we channel it, not just with songs and alarm clocks, but with all of our actions, MORE is attainable, rewarding and empowering.

In a similar manner, when it comes to retirement, John and Janet show that arriving at MORE is just having the right itinerary. The reality is that watching CNBC or trading stocks online doesn't make you a financial expert any more than standing in your garage makes you a car. It requires a plan - thoughtfully executed that can enable a greater level of satisfaction, personalization and success.

To quote a band from my teenaged past, the Red Hot Chili Peppers, "this life is MORE than just a read through." MORE is not a far off fantasy-land; it is in front of you, and you are worthy of its destination. Let's start walking today.

PROLOGUE

As you pick up this book, you may be asking yourself, "My retirement should be MORE *what*?" That's a great question.

We believe a large percentage of the population has pretty low and conventional expectations in just about every aspect of retirement. Our goal is to change that, to provoke an awakening about some of the nuances of retirement planning we believe can make a huge difference.

You may also be asking, "Is this book really for me? Can I learn any more than I already know about retirement?" After all, more has probably been said about the subject than any other aspect of personal finance. Well, let's see. Ask yourself these questions:

→ Do you have a *written* plan to provide regular, predictable, dependable income that will last the remainder of your life?

→ Do you have a strategy to adjust that income to allow you to keep pace with rising prices that will certainly happen after you retire?

→ Are you at all concerned another 2008 financial crisis in the market might vanquish your plans for a happy retirement?

→ Do you feel intimidated about the idea of living for the remainder of your days without the security of a steady paycheck?

→ Do you or your spouse have concerns about the ability to step up and handle the various aspects of your personal finances at the time of the other's death?

If any of these questions struck a chord with you, you've come to the right place. Even if you have another question about retirement that perplexes you, the *Power of MORE* may have your answers.

We know retirement can be confusing. Our goal is to cut through the confusion, help you get a clear vision of what retirement can be, and enable you to build toward financial independence.

So much rides on the success of the plans you make for what we like to call "Life 2.0," but so little is actually known as to how to achieve the outcomes many of you are looking for.

In our jobs of overseeing the financial future of the nearly 4,000 clients of our firm, we've learned a thing or two about what works (and what doesn't) when it comes to funding Life 2.0. This book is our attempt to help you put to work some of the things we've discovered along the way.

Your retirement should be MORE! Let us harness the *Power of MORE* for you!

CHAPTER 1

YOUR RETIREMENT SHOULD BE

MORE

PERSC

NAL

I f you have ever tried to figure out the puzzle we call "retire-ment planning," you might have found yourself overwhelmed. Ideally, you'd walk away from this experience with a feeling of confidence that you will one day be able to clock out of your job for the last time and live by your own means for the rest of your life. However, it rarely seems to feel that way. In many cases, you are left either struggling to figure it all out on your own or turning this incredibly important aspect of your life and finances over to someone else, hoping it all works out.

Hope is not a plan.

Failing to plan for retirement is like striking off on a trip with a specific deadline and destination but *having no idea the direction you need to go.*

Whether you look online or you happen to be among the select few who have a retirement income plan, you will likely find the focus is mostly on achieving some astronomical asset total or abiding by some mathematical "rule of thumb," which we like to call a "rule of dumb." You will find people promoting the philosophy that low expenses and high returns are the **only** factors that matter when it comes to investing your money for retirement. You will also likely find the ever-present industry promotion of "the good life," with photos of aging couples walking on the beach at sunset, hand-in-hand, and endless rounds of golf in some exotic location.

While there is nothing wrong with any of that, the realities of retirement center around the day-to-day need to meet your basic living expenses, the desire to enjoy experiences with grandchildren, the impact of increased unavoidable medical care that government programs like Medicare may not cover, and the desire to leave matters for your family in a better state than was left for you. These are some of the real needs and desires that confront people on the threshold of retirement, and it's why we say retirement should be *MORE about you!*

"Which of you, wishing to build a tower, does not first sit down and count the cost to see if he has the resources to complete it?" —Luke 14:28

Let's begin with what retirement *should* look like. Start by throwing away the cookie-cutter and doing the work of building a very specific, written plan to support the lifestyle *you* want to lead for the rest of your life. While the details of an ideal retirement plan will vary as widely as the personalities of each retiree, there are some common threads:

→ Income that is regular, predictable, and dependable to meet the everyday expenses of your life. Think of this as paycheck replacement.

→ Strategies to meet head-on the myriad of risks that are unique to retirees.

→ Safeguards to make sure you don't run out of money while you are still living the life you've designed.

→ Methods to increase your retirement paycheck periodically to make sure you don't fall behind in your ability to provide dignity and independence for yourself as prices rise during your retirement.

→ Your plan should also, if you so desire, include a strategy for leaving a legacy to your loved ones after you are gone.

These things, we believe, are fundamental to any retirement plan worth the paper it is printed on. Unfortunately, very few people have such a plan. Collectively, we have been helping people with their finances for more than 45 years. We have worked with thousands of clients and can tell you it is rare for us to see these basic elements in any plan those clients have brought in for us to review.

Let us share with you a story about how terribly wrong things can go if you don't get good advice before you embark on retirement. In 2007, a woman walked into our office seeking help. We will call her Linda, although that isn't her real name. Seven years earlier, Linda was so confident about her finances that she had decided to retire early, at age 50. Most people would agree she had *made it*, financially speaking. After a long and impressive career with a major communications company, she had more than $1.3 million in her company retirement plan. Linda did not live an extravagant lifestyle, so that amount seemed like plenty to take her through the next several decades. Linda's dream was to rely on her savings to enjoy life while she was still healthy enough to do so. Shortly after her retirement, however, some things went terribly wrong.

By the time she reached out to us in 2007, she was distraught. When we looked into her finances, we discovered that her retirement fund of $1.3 million was now worth only slightly more than $300,000. At age 57, Linda was on her way to being broke before she turned 60. The only advice we could give her was that she would have to return to work—and quickly—in order to make ends meet.

After all the joy and excitement she experienced, believing she was set for life only seven years earlier, she was now facing the prospect of reentering the workforce at an age when many find it very difficult to secure a good position in communications, or any other white-collar industry. Even worse, she had been out of work, even if voluntarily, for seven years, so her résumé was not exactly ideal. Linda left devastated.

What happened? Financially, there were a lot of technical things that took down Linda's dreams. Many people would blame her plight on the bad markets of 2000–2002, which started right at the beginning of her retirement. Others would say an exception to the retirement rules that allowed Linda to begin drawing from her retirement before the standard age of 59½ set her on the course toward failure. Some might even say Linda simply didn't have access to the information she needed to navigate retirement successfully. The truth is the failure of Linda's retirement plan was set *before* she took her first withdrawal and *before* she invested the first dollar. The advice she had received wasn't about ***her***!

As we dug deeper into Linda's situation, it was clear she had received truly terrible advice. There was just no strategy in place to address her basic needs throughout the course of her retirement. She received cookie-cutter advice that didn't take into account her specific needs and situation. Instead of securing regular, dependable income for Linda—the absolute baseline foundation of any retirement plan—her advisor had talked her into cashing in her pension and buying so-called hot stocks. Now, there are times when liquidating a pension might be appropriate. But, before you take a step like that, you have to define how you will create regular, predictable retirement income that meets your needs. If you're not going to do it through a pension (and that's what pensions are designed to do), then you need to ask: how *are* you going to do it?

The advisor could have made various recommendations to Linda, such as creating her own pension, which could have been successfully coupled with other instruments. It's possible he was a great investment advisor, gifted at seeing trends in the market. However, investment advice should never be about the advisor's gut feelings or gifts; it should be about the investor—*you*! It must account for your unique financial needs, protect against your unique risks, and provide peace of mind for your unique retirement. But, in this case, everything was tied to the market. When the market took a downward spin, this strategy was a recipe for disaster. Within your plan, you absolutely must have a way to give the market time to work itself out.

There had also been no cautionary advice that attempting to retire at age 50 greatly increased her chances of depleting her retirement assets quickly and disastrously. Like others who decide to retire before age 59½, there was a pre-determined Internal Revenue Service (IRS) calculation that controlled the income she would withdraw from her assets, and it could only have been changed *one time* before she reached age 60. In Linda's case, for a plethora of reasons, by the time she came to see us, that opportunity to change what she was drawing down wouldn't have put her in a better position anyway. Her money was running out, and she *couldn't* stop withdrawing it!

She was locked in until age 60. And, with $300,000 in the account, she was going to reach zero well before that. She was faced with the fact that, only seven years after walking out of her career, she was going to have to find work that could not only provide her with the income she needed (or was going to need) but also would build up enough savings to be able to retire again sometime in the future. It was one of the most difficult conversations we've ever had. Because there was no help we could provide, we're sorry to tell you we never saw Linda again. We hope she found a way to make her financial future work. We think about her often as the example of what should NEVER happen to someone during their retirement.

Could Linda's retirement have been successful had she been better informed? Should she have read her prospectus more carefully? (We'd never discourage you from reading a prospectus, but most people find them pretty confusing.) Linda found herself in the situation most pre-retirees face: drowning in information but starving for understanding.

How do we gain understanding about retirement planning? In many ways, the internet is a wonderful tool, because you can find out almost anything. If you can sift through all the endless data, you might find some truth, *but* information is a far cry from *understanding*. Beyond that, there's a further leap, which is *implementation*. Our belief is that understanding best comes through a relationship with a trusted advisor who clearly has your well-being at the forefront of what they do. An advisor can not only help you understand but also help you implement a plan based on your understanding. We've watched people struggle to go it alone and fail. Therefore, we believe developing a relationship with a skilled financial advisor is the best way for retirement planning to reach its potential.

How do you pick an advisor? We'll dig into that more in a later chapter, but rule number one comes from Dave Ramsey, national radio personality and financial guru, who says, "Pick an advisor who has the heart of a teacher." There is simply too much to understand for the average person to figure it out without the right kind of help. Remember: every great athlete has a coach. The coach doesn't deliver performance in the sense that they run, play, or train for athletes, but rather that they help athletes to perform better by giving them accountability and a greater understanding of their sport. It's not a sign of weakness or lack of wisdom to need a coach. Even Michael Jordan had a coach throughout his career!

And yet, the majority of people try to figure out retirement planning alone. A recent report from the Life Insurance Marketing and Research Association (LIMRA) showed that only 16 percent of the population had a formal, written retirement plan. That's a sobering statistic. This same study found that people who did have a written plan were more likely to feel confident that they were saving enough for retirement and more than twice as likely to feel very prepared for retirement, compared to those without one.

Why do we avoid planning for retirement? One reason, we believe, is exemplified perfectly by those TV ads you see of people walking around with giant Styrofoam numbers that represent the lump sum they *need* in order to retire comfortably. The part these ads get right is that everyone has individual needs and desires for retirement, so the numbers involved vary widely. However, the part they get wrong is the lump-sum concept. There are several different ways in which the lump sum you have is only a piece of the retirement puzzle, and we'll go into the financial reasons shortly. Moreover, we fear most people watching those ads are going to be thinking not only "I wonder what my number is?" (which is what the advertisers are hoping), but also "Oh my goodness! I have nowhere near any of those numbers! My retirement is going to be a disaster!! I can't deal with this right now!!!"

If we don't change this trend, we will continue to see Americans heading into this time of their lives woefully unprepared and underserved by both the industry and the government that regulates it. Think of that investor like a teenager who is about to reach the legal driving age. Imagine for a moment that she's never taken driver's ed, and her parents simply hand her the keys to the family car and say, "Good luck!" That teen would be set up for failure, and the howls

"Imagine for a moment that one's parents simply hand that young person the keys to the family car and, with a nod to the need for training, toss them the owner's manual, saying 'Good luck!'"

of outrage from society would be deafening! Yet, many treat their own retirement with a similar lack of preparation. Our goal is to give you a ride-along driving coach. You know, the type of coach who tells you to look out for all the things that might not happen but could. The one who, through years of experience, knows many of the curves, speedbumps, blind spots, and distractions you may come upon the road and can keep you focused as you drive safely to your destination. Success in retirement planning is found where information and understanding intersect with implementation. And, the roadmap to get you there is found in the office of a trustworthy financial advisor. If you are headed toward retirement, you're already in the car. So, buckle up, and let's roll!

In this book, we'll be diving into several factors that would have made for a radically different, and much happier, outcome for Linda.

The real takeaway we want you to have is that Linda's story *could have been different*. For her, it was too late, but it doesn't have to be that way for you.

Retirement should be the grand finale of your life, following years of working for a living, raising kids, caring for elderly parents, and having your actions and decisions heavily dictated by the needs of others. In short, it should be ***your time***, when everything comes together to make the focus about ***your*** needs. We call that *"harnessing the Power of MORE!"*

→ **Reject "homogenized" and embrace customized advice.** Cookie-cutters are kitchen utensils, not tools for retirement planning. Marketing has caused the proliferation of "rules of dumb" that sound good but do little to move you toward your goals. Your life is unique. Your financial plan should be too.

→ **All that glitters is not gold.** It seems that every year has a "hot investment" many believe will make them a millionaire. Rarely does that happen. Don't be distracted by "the shiny things" of the investment world. Often, they are hot until they are not. And when they are not, it can spell disaster for your financial future.

→ **Spend the time; get help.** You probably won't tackle a more important financial decision than setting yourself up to have a quality lifestyle when you are ready to quit the grind of the 9 to 5. Nor are there many challenges more daunting. First, make the commitment to yourself to deal with it. Next, find a financial coach who will support you and use their expertise to get you there.

CHAPTER 2

YOUR RETIREMENT SHOULD BE

MORE DEPEND

ABLE

Retirement is essentially an income problem, not an

asset problem.

Common sense tells us that unless you understand the true nature of a problem, you won't be very successful at solving it. By focusing on the wrong aspect of retirement, many people either struggle with or become discouraged by their efforts to build a successful plan. Without question, hundreds of millions of dollars have been spent to encourage Americans to work toward their *big number* for retirement. Recently, a survey by the Employee Benefit Retirement Institute and a study by Legg Mason, an investment management company, revealed the estimates needed to finance the average worker's retirement lifestyle are anywhere from $250,000 to $2.5 million. This extensive range has clearly confounded many baby boomers, who have been busy financing their *current* lifestyle while simultaneously trying to set aside what they can for the future. Focusing on these seemingly insurmountable estimates can be intimidating, and giving attention to an undefined *big number* is misguided.

Allow us to illustrate it this way: Suppose you come home one day to find a large chunk of gold the size of a small car sitting in your backyard. With gold prices (as of this writing) above $1,000 per ounce, owning this large chunk of it would make you very wealthy. But, if you had no income and needed to buy groceries tomorrow, you'd have to come up with a way to turn a portion of that gold into cash because Kroger doesn't accept precious metals at the register. Obviously, you have to accumulate assets in order to produce income in retirement, but many people have never examined exactly how much income they will need.

So, why do people get so caught up on a lump-sum number? For some, it seems to start from the day they sign up for their 401(k) plan.

"Suppose you come home one day to find a large chunk of gold the size of a small car sitting in your back yard."

You probably know the drill. You go to your new job and visit the human resources department. The nice lady hands you a packet of information about the 401(k) plan and says, "Have it back by Friday."

And, that's it.

From what our clients tell us, that is the only *training* they have regarding this important investment vehicle. Somewhere in that packet is a graphic that shows if you set aside X number of dollars over your working lifetime, you will have *big number Y* as a lump sum when you retire. And so begins the focus on the *big number*.

We don't believe focusing on the *big number* works for retirement planning. In retirement, it is critical to have predictable, dependable income regardless of market conditions. Your monthly expenses have a tendency to be both predictable and dependable. The utility company will continue to bill you every month, even though you retired. Food will still need to be bought, and houses still need repairs. It's necessary to have a certain amount of what we call "required income" to meet those predictable expenses. We believe this must be *Job Number 1* when it comes to retirement planning. Therefore, instead of focusing on a nebulous *big number*, we want you to focus on your *monthly number*.

Almost every client who has entered our office has asked us, "How much money do I need to be able to retire?"

Our answer is always the same: "It depends."

We coach people on the concept of income replacement or paycheck replacement. You are seeking to make work either optional or unnecessary, so you've got to focus on HOW to replace that paycheck. How much you need to accumulate for retirement depends on factors like:

→ Your monthly income needs to meet your expense obligations

→ Your Social Security benefit amount

→ Your debt obligations

→ Your other guaranteed income sources

That's why one of the first questions we ask an investor who comes to us is, "What is your current income need per month?" This seemingly straightforward question has produced a surprisingly high number of blank stares over our many years meeting with clients. Often, the silence is deafening as we wait for their response. With some, it's as if we are dealing with a foreign concept. We are determined, however, to have a clear understanding of their income needs now because we want to clearly define what their required income needs will be in retirement. We do not, however, subscribe to these formulas that guide you to plan on spending 70 percent to 90 percent of your existing income in retirement. It's not about a formula; it's about *you*.

Individuals have a wide range of visions regarding how retirement should or could look. That's why, from the beginning, you need to know what your *monthly number (required income)* is and work from there.

There's a difference between dreaming about your desired lifestyle and knowing about your required income. To that end, we have to have a forward-looking conversation about what your life looks like when you retire. Obviously, you've got to eat and pay the electric bill before you can take that trip to Tahiti. You also need to include more than the bare basics like food, clothing, and transportation. Many items that used to be considered luxuries, such as cell phones and cable service, are now an essential part of life, so you need to include them. Finally, you will need to factor in changes that reduce your expenses, such as finishing off your mortgage or selling the home where you raised a family and possibly moving to somewhere smaller and more cost-efficient.

To illustrate why a focus on the *monthly number* is key, let us share with you a meeting we had recently with a couple in their 40s who received a windfall of $100,000. It's important to know they had a relatively small amount of money saved for their retirement, but both are professionals and presumably had a number of years to continue to work on their retirement savings. They had several ideas regarding how they might enjoy this unexpected cash, but their focus wasn't on retirement. The husband was really intent on trying his hand at some discretionary investing—chasing some investment ideas and hot stocks. The conversation went like this:

We asked: "Have you taken care of your first priority yet?"

He said: "What's that?"

We said: "Your base retirement income—the money you will need to replace your paycheck when you retire?"

Crickets

This couple had been contributing to their 401(k) accounts but, at that time, were not on track to replace their paychecks, and many of their existing expenses would still be there during retirement. With those goals in mind, they really needed to dedicate most of the $100,000 toward their future retirement needs.

It was crystal clear this hadn't even occurred to them. If this guy had done what he was instinctively driven to do, he might have had a good return or he might not. Or in the future, he might have found something he wanted to spend that money on, all the while failing to focus on *Job Number 1*: making sure he and his wife had the *required income* to cover their basic living expenses in retirement.

Here's another example. Janet had a recent visit with a couple in their 50s who were about to replace their vehicle and wanted to withdraw $25,000 from their retirement assets so they wouldn't have to worry about car payments. Many would agree that avoiding debt is a smart idea. Depending on current interest rates and the assets available, it may be a wise decision; however, in this case, the money would have had to come from their retirement assets, not from savings.

All of their retirement assets are needed to generate the predictable, dependable income they'll need for retirement, which was not too far down the road. If they withdrew that $25,000 now, it would reduce their income, and they'd likely earn that back. Janet suggested they protect their retirement savings and use monthly income to make the car payments. She understood the desire to avoid car payments and that making sure the payments are kept up is yet another administrative chore. However, there are times when the reduction in assets can impact your future income potential too drastically. A retirement nest egg is like a milk cow. If you kill the cow in order to have steak, you eat steak for a few days, but the milk is gone forever.

Now that we have discussed the importance of predictable and dependable income, what's next? You need to assess the resources you have available to provide that predictable, dependable income to meet those expenses. With pensions being phased out by employers across the country, most people will find that their only source for predictable, dependable income during retirement is Social Security. Let's say you've calculated a good estimate of the income you'll need in retirement, and it's about $5,000 a month for the essentials. For this example, let's say you and your spouse together can bring in $4,000 from your Social Security benefits.

Expenses	$5,000
Income	$4,000
SHORTFALL	**$1,000**

Remember, *Job Number 1* in retirement income planning is deciding how to use your other assets to make up any shortfall you may have in meeting your required expenses. In this example, the shortfall is $1,000 of *additional* predictable, dependable cash needed to allow your income—at an absolute minimum—to *equal* your expenses.

Once you have taken care of *Job Number 1* and your income needs have been protected through predictable, dependable sources, the next task is ensuring there are safeguards in place to protect your remaining assets while you live the life you designed. Many of the conventional methods for achieving this are faulty from the start. Most methods rely on a flat withdrawal percentage paired with an average rate of return, which simply doesn't work in the real world. For example, if your portfolio experienced a loss, could you afford to simply lower your monthly distribution proportionally? Moreover, the idea of average returns can be misleading. We like to use a demonstration in our workshops to illustrate this point.

We ask our colleague Charlie (who is 6'4") to stand beside Janet (who is 5'3"), and we point out that Charlie is above average in height, while Janet's height is below average. The trouble is that, if you put their heights together and calculate an average (5'8½"), neither of them is actually that *average* height. It's the same with investment returns. You can look at an investment that has an *average* return, hypothetically, of 7 percent over a period of twenty years. However, when you take a look at the returns year by year, you might find that this investment performed way above or way below the 7 percent average in any given year. You could find that it *never* actually returned 7 percent in any of those years. What's even more misleading about a focus on average returns is that extreme fluctuations in returns could cause you to run out of money *before* you run out of time.

We teach our clients about this by showing them an example of two people who retired with exactly the same amount of money, invested in the exact same portfolio (60 percent stocks/40 percent bonds) and took the same amount of income from their investments, adjusting regularly for inflation. However, there is ONE difference between them: the first person retired in 1966, the other in 1976.

Due to the order (or sequence) of the market returns experienced by the first investor, he ended up exhausting his life savings 16 years after he retired. The second retiree had the good fortune of having mostly favorable investment returns over the course of his lifetime, so his initial investment of $500,000 grew to more than $2.5 million *even after having taken income from the portfolio over the entire 30 years.* The only difference, remember, was how the markets performed during each of their respective retirement years.

So, here's the question: do you know what kind of returns you can expect right before and during your retirement? Of course not! No one can predict the course of the markets over a short time period. The time period immediately before and after your retirement date is critical as it relates to your success and financial survival. Therefore, we believe you MUST have a strategy to address this sequence of return risk.

A strategy we have used for a number of years with our clients, the *GenWealth Ready-to-Retire Process*, involves breaking down a client's total investment dollars into buckets, or segments, with different investment objectives for each bucket. This allows us to manage risk and exposure to the stock market with funds that will be utilized for income during the first years of retirement while seeking growth opportunities for funds that will have time to use market volatility to their benefit.

We know the odds of losing money in the market in any given one-year period are roughly 40 percent. If you are withdrawing money when that losing year rolls around, it just makes your portfolio lose that much more value. We also know the odds of losing money in the stock market have historically decreased the longer you stay invested. In fact, the market as measured by the S&P 500 has had only one 10-year period since 1972 with a negative return. When you stretch out your holding period to 20 years, the worst the market has performed is 6.4 percent. Clearly, the market is telling us that when you buy stocks, you should have a very long-term view. That's why we assign the equity investments to the longer time horizons and use safer, less volatile investments to fund the first years of income when we design a retirement portfolio. (The folks who watch over our industry would have us add that *past performance is not indicative of future results*, and none of these examples reflect the performance of an actual investment.)

When retirees are selling from a portfolio to create income, we believe that using the *GenWealth Ready-to-Retire Process* decreases their sequence of return risk due to naturally occurring market fluctuation. We don't encourage chasing a greater rate of return, which ultimately no one can control. Attempting to beat the market and comparing returns tends to cause many people to lose sight of the *outcome* they are seeking: a sufficient income that lasts them the rest of their lives.

So, let us be clear. What counts in retirement is income—*your* income. You've depended on it all your adult life, one way or another, and retirement isn't really any different. There should be **more** to retirement than just hoping you can meet your required expenses. Retirement planning is all about retirement income, and you deserve MORE than just a vague number to work toward. A trustworthy advisor can help you clearly define your retirement income needs and develop a strategy to provide dependable, predictable income to meet them.

➔ **Think paycheck replacement rather than "the big number."** Most of us have spent our entire lives living on an employer's salary. Retirement is no different. You will have monthly bills that you have to pay off with monthly income. Creating a plan to provide for that monthly income can increase your chances of avoiding spending your lump sum of retirement savings and running out of money before you run out of time.

➔ **Create your customized spending plan for your retirement years.** It doesn't have to be "to the penny" precise, but you do need to have a good idea of how much it costs you to run your household and your life on a monthly basis. Once you get that number, remember to increase it to account for taxes you will need to pay if you are going to be spending pretax money from accounts like your individual retirement account (IRA), 401(k), or pension.

→ **Decide if you want to count on a *probabilities* strategy or a *safety-first* strategy.** Some advisors advocate "playing the odds" when it comes to retirement income. They design income plans that have something less than a 100 percent **probability** of being able to survive through your lifetime. Ask yourself if you are OK with having, say, an 80 percent chance of your retirement funds lasting as long as you do? Or, would you be more comfortable with a *safety-first* strategy that ensures the income will be there for the rest of your life? The *GenWealth Ready-to-Retire Process* is an example of a *safety-first* strategy.

CHAPTER 3

YOUR RETIREMENT SHOULD BE MORE STRATEG

Ask anyone about their retirement plan, and they will likely start talking about the investments (and the performance thereof) that they are using *in* their plan. Probe a little bit further, and you will likely find their investments *are* their plan. In essence, a vast majority of Americans unwittingly believe that if they have a 401(k) or IRA, they have a *plan* for their life after work. It's time to expand our thinking.

Retirement is MORE than just investments!

Our advisors characterize retirement as "a 30-year vacation." Utilizing this analogy of a vacation, the role of investments in your retirement plan is much like that of a car on your annual two-week vacation. Investments are simply a vehicle that can get you there if cared for properly, but many people spend more time working on plans for their two-week family trips than their future retirement. To succeed in retirement requires that we give careful consideration to our vehicles and consider the bumps we may encounter along our path. You must do much more than throw dollars into a proverbial pile over your working lifetime, then siphon off funds once you quit work. This idea of a 30-year retirement timeline presents a myriad of challenges and possibilities. Let's explore a couple of these in more detail.

As a group, we are living longer, and threats to our health remain a top concern. Increased awareness of health and advances in medicine are stretching life expectancy to new levels. Most think that living long is a good thing, but adding years to your life adds stress to your portfolio. The longer you live, the more important it is for you to have a strategy to ensure that your income lives as long as you do. Despite this trend, Merrill Lynch and Age Wave conducted a study that found 81 percent of respondents ranked good health as the most important factor of a happy retirement. The study also revealed

"Our advisors characterize retirement as 'a 30-year vacation.'"

that retirees fear things like Alzheimer's and dementia. Preparing for long-term health issues continues to be a challenge with only one-fifth of those age 65 or older carrying chronic care insurance.

We don't want to live our parents' retirement. When "the greatest generation" retired, they hung up their work clothes and settled in for a life at home, waiting for the kids and grandkids to visit. Dictionary.com uses the word "withdraw" to describe retirement, but retirees now are viewing retirement as simply another phase of their lives. Today, our retiring clients tell us travel experiences are their number-one desire after they quit work. Retirees are more active than ever and are fueling a boom in the leisure industry. Seven in ten pre-retirees tell us they plan to work during their retirement, but they plan to work differently. The new normal is doing something for the love of it, rather than for the paycheck.

But, if retirement planning isn't simply compiling funds in investments to later pull from, why does that seem to be the focus when you look around? The focus on the investment portion of the retirement equation is rooted in an attempt to simplify what can be a very confusing and complex problem. Investments are seemingly easy to quantify. It is natural for us to latch on to things we can measure, and it would appear that focusing on the return and expenses of investments would make it easy. Look for the biggest number when it comes to returns and the lowest number when it comes to expenses, and you're done. Unfortunately, a successful retirement strategy requires much more.

Even many advisors can't see the forest for the trees. Take a tour of most advisor websites, and you will see a great deal of focus on investment management and performance but not much help in navigating the complexities we've discussed about retirement. There are thousands of websites and at least two cable TV channels devoted to breathless, play-by-play commentary about the market and "what you should do today." Even on your smartphone, you can find apps with information, direction, and opinions on investments. With all these voices shouting investment returns and costs as supreme, it might surprise you to know that the experts on the subject of retirement say this focus is all wrong.

David Littell and Jamie Hopkins lead the Retirement Income program at the American College of Financial Services. Their article in the October 2015 issue of *Journal of Financial Planning* explained that typically two out of three Americans talk with their financial advisor at least twice per year and rely on them heavily to manage their finances. However, their research concluded that just one in four Americans have a formal written retirement plan. This same article pointed out that selecting the right investments is not your most important decision in retirement.

So, if expenses and returns are the wrong focus for retirement success, what things should be the focus? Let's discuss a few in more detail:

1. **Cash-flow management:** Cash-flow management is making sure that you are directing your dollars where you want and need them to go. The direction of your dollars should be determined by the outcomes you are seeking. For most people, this is one of the more difficult steps of planning. Because it's not exciting and it requires (in most cases) some degree of behavior modification on the part of the individual, advisors often shy away from this critical area. That doesn't make it any less important. *Cash-flow management is the fuel for the vehicle on your retirement journey.*

2. **Debt management:** Debt is a drain on the income streams you will establish in retirement. Eliminating debt for retirement is a plan that begins *before* you retire. It does **not** mean reaching into your 401(k) to pay off all debt. True debt management utilizes wisdom to determine which expenses need to be eliminated prior to retirement and which expenses can be part of cash-flow management.

3. **Tax management:** Conventional wisdom favors investing in pretax and tax-deferred instruments because of the

long-term benefits of keeping Uncle Sam's hands off your retirement dollars and because of the assumption that taxes will be lower for you when you retire. However, lower taxes are not a given, and we have seen many retirees frustrated that every dime of their income from 401(k)/IRA money is taxable to them as ordinary income when they retire.

Additionally, they aren't happy that as much as 85 percent of their Social Security benefits are taxable as well! Because retirement is a time when a lot of folks have paid off their houses and their kids have grown up and out of the house, retirees become sitting ducks for the tax man because they have few, if any, deductions. Changes to the tax laws that took effect in late 2018 make it even more unlikely that retirees will be able to itemize because of the increase in the standard deduction. However, there are strategies, like utilizing Roth IRAs, that can help alleviate some of this tax pressure in retirement.

4. **Efficient income structuring:** Knowing when and how to tap into sources of income in retirement is important. Understanding pensions, Social Security, and how to sequence taking dollars from investment accounts can

maximize your retirement income or drain it if handled poorly. There are more than eighty claiming strategies available for Social Security, yet many don't even know there are options. They simply start their benefits and hope it will work. Again, hope is not a plan. Making the wrong move regarding how to sequence your income for retirement can cost you hundreds of thousands of dollars!

5.   **Survivor income protection:** What happens to your Social Security and pension income when you die? Did you know that a married couple on Social Security will likely take a substantial hit to their cash flow when one spouse dies? Like Social Security, many pensions offer multiple withdrawal options. They can vary from a single-life option to a full joint and survivor benefit. On one end, your survivor would not receive any income from your pension at all if you were to predecease them; on the other end, the full joint and survivor benefit would provide continued income in your absence. Consider the effect of a substantial loss of income for your surviving spouse, and you will understand why this is a critical aspect of retirement planning.

6.   **Preparing to pass it on:** Benjamin Franklin is credited with saying, "The only things certain in life are death and taxes."

According to LexisNexis, more than half of us will die without a will or any other type of estate plan. Some have the attitude of "Why should I care? I'll be dead." We believe you should know that estate planning isn't for you; it's for your *family*. Ignoring estate planning is like leaving a big mess everywhere you go. It's a major burden for someone to clean up. Passing away without an estate plan can cost your family lots of money and potentially delay access to your hard-earned resources at a time when they may need them the most.

While most of these six areas can and should be addressed earlier in life, there is no time more critical to address them than as you approach retirement. However, it appears our near obsession with the rate of return and fees has us taking our eye off the ball. That doesn't mean investments don't matter at all. As we mentioned previously, they are the vehicle that takes us to our 30-year vacation called retirement. When we counsel clients about investing, we focus on certain factors that affect long-term goal success. Like making sure your car is maintained before a long trip, your retirement plan requires care. Here are three critical factors when it comes to caring for your investment vehicle:

1. **Plan-oriented savings:** Maximizing your employer match is, of course, an important piece of your retirement savings

puzzle. It is not, however, a stand-alone fix for retirement funding. We have previously discussed the urgency of creating a unique plan for your retirement. Once you know what your plan is for retirement income, set your spending and saving habits around that plan. And as a reminder, this plan needs to account for the six factors we discussed above. A qualified financial advisor worth his or her salt will be able to help you calculate your savings needs based on your plan goals.

2. **Segmented investments:** In chapter 2, we discussed the strategy that we use with our clients, which involves breaking down a client's portfolio into time-segmented buckets to invest. We do this to manage risk exposure and volatility for funds that will be used in earlier years of retirement while seeking opportunities for later sources of income. A segmented approach also helps an investor spread his investments over multiple categories and classes.

3. **Staying on course:** You can obviously tell we are big advocates for planning. In fact, the mantra in our financial practice is "Prescription without diagnosis is malpractice." But almost as bad as not planning at all is tossing the plan out the window when short-term circumstances change. The biblical principle

found in Luke 9:62 is our guide here: "No man who puts his hand to the plow and looks back is fit for the Kingdom of God." Your financial plan should be your North Star, your base when times get rocky and uncomfortable. Investment decisions should be made based on the plan, not emotional highs and lows. We've been around enough to know that investments come and go with a wide variety of results, but those who depend on their plan and have a financial coach to help them stay on track tend to have better outcomes and feel more confident in their future.

Here's some unconventional wisdom: **People generally don't botch retirement because they picked the wrong investment. They do so because they didn't have a plan.** They thought they had one, but they either found that it was misguided or they abandoned the plan when things went sideways.

Obsessing about finding the right stocks or bonds to be used in your plan is, in our opinion, far less meaningful than the financial press would have you believe. We believe buying the cheapest fund is of very little benefit if that fund doesn't provide the outcome you are looking for. Harnessing the *Power of MORE* with your investments means matching the investments in your plan with the purpose you have pre-determined for the money.

→ **Your retirement is more important than your vacation.** We get it. Planning a vacation is fun. Planning retirement can seem like swimming in deep water without a life vest. We don't advocate eschewing the family trip for a singular focus on retirement, but we do believe you should allocate more of your time to your "permanent vacation" than a temporary one.

→ **Your investments do not constitute your "plan."** Just because you participate in your company's 401(k) plan doesn't mean *you have a plan*. You have investments, and that is a good first step. The MORE factor is how those investments can be utilized to create a lifestyle for yourself, and it can't just be in your head. You've got to take your ideas from "vapor to paper" and focus on the outcomes you are looking for.

→ **Become a "dollar director."** It seems as though money has a mind of its own, and unless we take control of it, it goes wherever it wants. Ask yourself, "Where do I want it to go? What do I want it to do?" What are your priorities? Reducing debt, managing taxes, creating income, and passing along financial security to your family are all worthy goals. Direct your dollars accordingly, and you will have the foundational concept of a good plan under your control.

CHAPTER 4

YOUR RETIREMENT SHOULD BE MORE CERTAIN

Most of us remember the teeter-totter in grade school. The trick was to get a partner on the other end who was about your same weight, so there would be a balance as the two of you went up and down. But you knew you were in for problems if one of the bigger kids decided he wanted to be on the other end of the see-saw while you were riding. If you've got that image in your mind, you have a pretty good idea of the relationship between your retirement income and your expenses.

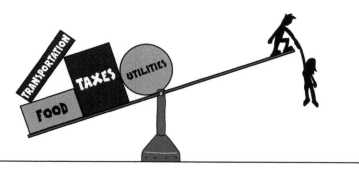

"Most of us remember the teeter-totter at our grade school. If you've got that image in your mind, you have a pretty good idea of the relationship between your retirement income and your expenses."

On one side of the scale, you've got your monthly liabilities: things like food, clothing, transportation costs, housing expenses, taxes, and insurance. Think about the basic expenses that won't go away during your retirement. On the other side of the scale are the sources of your regular, predictable, dependable income: your monthly assets, which should offset the monthly liabilities. This would include things like Social Security and pensions. We call the amount of money needed to meet those liabilities your *required income*.

When you go through the basic mathematics of this monthly balance sheet, you will quickly find out if you have sufficient income or a shortfall, which we call a "gap" in your retirement income strategy. So, let's explore what that looks like and some of the challenges you might face. First, you would be surprised at the number of people we see in our practice each week who are headed for retirement but have never taken the time to determine how much money will need to be deposited into their checking account each month to pay their bills.

Creating a spending plan is not hard, but it ranks right up there with cleaning out the gutters as the activity you would least like to do on your day off. But if you don't know what you will need, you have no way of knowing whether you will be able to sustain your retirement for the rest of your life. It's an exercise you only need to do once, then make small adjustments along the way as your expenses change. Once you have a clear picture of your required expenses, you can then turn your attention to the assets you have to meet those expenses. This is where things can become challenging because the landscape of reliable sources of retirement income is changing very rapidly.

As late as 1979, four in ten people could say they could rely on a monthly check in the form of a pension payment from their former employer. Today, only about one in ten private-sector workers has access to a pension, and that number is decreasing every year. The change has largely been driven by two factors: the push to cut corporate expenses and the rise of the 401(k) plan. Pensions are very expensive to the companies that sponsor them. Over the years, companies found those expenses had become too much for them to continue to bear, and they began to move away from those valuable programs. Today pension plans are offered by only a few of the larger employers in America and to federal, state, and local government workers. Many of those pension plans are in financial trouble, facing unfunded liabilities and dwindling revenue.

The 401(k) plan came along to provide an avenue for employees to build some additional retirement savings from their own paycheck. Also, the 401(k) plan answered an inherent problem with pensions, which was a lack of portability for employees who were changing jobs (as today's workers do more often than previous generations). Then, employers began to shift their contributions away from pensions and to the 401(k) plans as match and profit-sharing incentives. This has had the effect of placing the burden of managing those accounts on employees, most of whom have no training or expertise to do so.

Our parents relied on retirement income from a combination of pensions and Social Security. Obviously, pensions are all but gone, and Social Security faces, at the very least, a crisis in confidence—and at worst, a financial collapse. When Social Security started, there were ten workers contributing to the system for every person receiving benefits. Today, according to the Social Security Administration, the ratio is fewer than three to one. The Social Security government website, SSA.gov, reports that if no changes are made to the system by 2032, there will have to be a 25 percent reduction in benefits. Very few people whom we see in our practice believe the program will continue in its current form. A 25 percent reduction in benefits could be devastating to many people for whom Social Security benefits make up a significant percentage of overall income.

So, here's the situation most retirees face: fixed monthly expenses that will likely increase with inflation while their uncertain sources of income—including Social Security, the bedrock that retirees have historically depended upon—dwindle away.

What we believe you would like to have is *more certainty.* Having sources of predictable and dependable income is key, in our opinion, to a successful retirement. The task at hand is transforming the lump sums of money you have accumulated through your savings efforts over the years into income streams you can live on for the rest of your life. But, as we mentioned, most people have no training regarding how to make that transition and to be sure they won't run out of money before they run out of time. It is at this point that your relationship with a well-trained, experienced financial advisor may help you create more certainty about your future income.

We believe there are **three big risks** that pose threats to your retirement. These are risks you did not have to deal with during the time when you were saving money, but now you are playing a different game and have to play by a different set of rules.

The three big risks:

→ **Retiring at the wrong time**

→ **Being overwhelmed by inflation**

→ **Outliving your money**

On the surface, these risks may seem somewhat out of your control, but we believe planning and strategy can help you overcome many of the issues that could create havoc with your retirement dreams. Of course, no strategy can ensure success, and life itself is a risk. The idea would be to reduce the risks as much as possible and, as we like to say, "Stack as many cards in your favor as you can." Let's dig a little deeper into each of these risks and discuss why they are important to manage.

Retiring at the wrong time: If you recall, in chapter 2, the illustration we shared about the two guys who retired with the same amount of money, just ten years apart, you will understand the problem of retiring at the wrong time. To refresh your memory, one person ran out of money in about 18 years while the other actually grew his account balance in spite of his withdrawals. In both cases, their results were determined by the time in history at which they retired and the market returns that followed their retirement. Obviously, there is no way to predict the future of market performance, but strategically allocating a portion of your retirement dollars to investments that are insulated in one way or another from market risks can help you avoid drawing money from a depreciating asset when the market is in turmoil.

Being overwhelmed by inflation: If you are fortunate enough to have a pension, chances are the payments are a fixed amount for the rest of your life. There is no increase for inflation in many of the private sector pension plans we have observed. Social Security superficially prescribes a "cost-of-living" adjustment to their benefits program; however, those increases are often offset by the increases in premiums for Medicare Part B, thereby having little to no increase in your spendable income. A certainty of retirement is that many of the things you will buy on a regular basis will cost more in the future than they do now. You should ask yourself how you will keep up with those rising costs. Building into your plan *a strategy* that will allow you to take more income at periodic future dates is one way to address this risk.

Outliving your money: This risk is probably one of the most concerning to those who stand at the threshold of retirement. To be aged and broke with very few options to generate income is not a fate anyone wants to face, yet life expectancies are increasing thanks to advances in medicine and people becoming increasingly health conscious. Living longer is a good thing, but one of the side effects of a long life is the pressure it puts on your retirement savings to support your lifestyle during that extended time. That's why your retirement income plan should employ a strategy to provide for a long life expectancy.

Each of these risks must be addressed; that is an indisputable fact. We believe there are essentially four ways to address *any* type of risk.

First, you can *avoid* it. However, trying to avoid the specific risks of retirement is difficult because by avoiding one risk you expose yourself to others. For example, you could decide the market is too risky and you're not going to invest. You decide you're going to save your money at the bank instead. Well, now you've avoided market risk, but you've accepted inflation risk because it's very likely inflation will outpace what you earn at the bank.

The second method of addressing risk is to simply *accept* the risk. This method is also foolhardy for all except the super wealthy because only the super wealthy have enough money to sustain a level of essential income without the fear of running out of capital.

The third method is to *transfer* the risk. This is what you do with your home, as an example. You have homeowners' insurance. Here in Little Rock, tornadoes are quite common, so you don't want to go without insurance. Whether you've paid off the mortgage on your home or not, you don't want to be in the position of paying to replace the house if it gets blown to pieces in a tornado. Instead, you transfer the risk to an insurance company, and you pay them to take on that risk.

The fourth method is to *manage* the risk. Managing the risk does not eliminate it, but it can lessen the probability of a large negative impact. Managing risk involves creating a plan that provides multiple sources of income so that if one portion of your assets is facing volatility, you aren't forced to utilize that portion and withdraw from a depreciating asset. It also involves having portions of your assets allocated to investments that have different objectives and exposures, as we have mentioned when we discussed the time-segmented buckets approach. But those methods require ongoing attention and caretaking, the kind that can be provided by a financial advisor well experienced in retirement income planning.

Attempting to avoid or simply accept risk when it comes to

your source of retirement income is unwise. We believe transferring and managing risk are acceptable methods of dealing with the **three big risks** in retirement, and any good retirement income plan will use these methods in a way that is specifically designed to your circumstances to mitigate some of the uncertainties you may face. Life happens even in retirement, but with the right plan and safeguards in place, you can increase the odds of experiencing **more certainty**!

→ **What does your retirement income "balance sheet" look like?** Compare your monthly expenses with the sources of "guaranteed" income you have access to. If there is a shortfall (or gap), then explore the variety of avenues available to fill that gap with a portion of the money you have saved for retirement. Like the foundation of a house, your "floor" of predictable income sources provides stability to the rest of your cash flow.

→ **At the point of retirement, the game changes.** You deal with one set of risks as you try to accumulate money for retirement. When you retire, the **three big risks** step to the forefront and present a whole new set of planning challenges. Be sure the plan for your retirement income adequately addresses each of these risks.

➔ **Get comfortable with the facts of Social Security.** You may be thinking, "Social Security won't be there when I get to retirement." But there is scant evidence of this scenario. If nothing changes, the SSA says benefits might have to be *reduced* by 2032. If you want to play it safe, use 75 percent of your current benefit to plan with. If nothing changes, you'll be ready. If Congress *does the right thing* and fixes the system as they did in the 1970s, you will have substantially more income than you expected. Don't fall victim to the fatalistic thinking that you will never draw a check. Such a scenario isn't very likely, and it certainly doesn't do anything for your attitude toward retirement.

CHAPTER 5

YOUR RETIREMENT SHOULD BE **MORE PREPAR**

D

Get a husband and wife in a room together as they approach retirement, and we can tell you they would rather talk about *anything* more than their long-term healthcare needs. It's a problem so daunting that even the most realistic person struggles to come to terms with the thought of their declining health and being dependent upon others to take care of them. Many of those we're talking about know the realities of this situation firsthand. They are part of what has been dubbed the "sandwich generation"—people who have been spread thin between raising their kids and caring for their elderly parents. Many have seen their parents suffer from dementia, Alzheimer's disease, or a variety of physical ailments to the point of not being able to care for them. Home healthcare or nursing home care become their only options.

"There, but for the grace of God, go I."

Statistics show that if a couple reaches age 65 and are fairly healthy, there is a high likelihood one of them will reach age 90. But, during that 25-year stretch, there is also a better than 50 percent chance that

"Get a husband and wife in a room together as they approach retirement, and we can tell you that they would rather talk about anything more than their long-term healthcare needs."

their health will decline to the point that they will need some type of long-term care. Fidelity Benefits Consulting also indicates that a couple retiring in 2017 at age 65 will need an average of $260,000 to cover medical expenses during their retirement. The lack of understanding regarding this complex problem places people in an even more precarious situation.

Commonly, we find there is a great deal of confusion about what aspects of healthcare are covered by Medicare (which nearly everyone in the United States qualifies for), Medicare supplement coverage, Medicaid (which is an income-based program operated at the state level), and long-term care insurance.

Medicare is simply health insurance for those age 65 and older and the disabled. It covers *acute care* needs such as doctor's visits, hospitalization, prescription drugs, and short-term rehabilitation. Medicare does *not* cover nursing home care or many of the other aspects of chronic and critical care needs.

Medicare Supplement coverage, purchased from private insurers, is designed to fill the gaps in acute care where Medicare falls short. There are numerous coverage options and varieties of these plans, but again, Medicare Supplement coverage offers *no* coverage for long-term care needs.

Medicaid is a program administered by the states, which ***does*** cover nursing home care but only ***for those with less than a couple thousand dollars*** in assets to their name. Let that soak in for a moment. It is the coverage of last resort because qualifying requires such a depleted financial state—and, frankly, the quality of care at a Medicaid facility is often less than what families would want for their loved ones. Some people are under the mistaken impression that you can qualify for Medicaid by transferring your wealth to other family members, but this tactic is problematic at best. States have mechanisms in place to "unwind" and void any transfer of wealth within a five-year period of time prior to a loved one having a need Medicaid would have otherwise covered. This is commonly known as a "look-back period." Dealing with this regulation has given rise to a whole subset of attorneys who specialize in trying to make arrangements ahead of time to protect the assets of an elderly person. They attempt to shield their assets and income, often with irrevocable trusts, from the Medicaid look-back rules so that their clients might qualify for coverage under the program.

Long-term care insurance is an insurance product that helps pay for certain costs associated with long-term care. Long-term care is available for people with chronic illnesses or disabilities, who need assistance with daily living activities over an extended period of time. Long-term care policies offer many different coverage options and have varying qualifying requirements.

People tend to fall into one of three categories in the discussion of long-term care needs. First, there are those who have a large amount of money and can self-pay for their long-term care coverage over and above their family's retirement income needs. Second, are the people who have very limited resources and will end up qualifying for Medicaid after either spending what they have on their care and falling on the mercy of the state, or by using the elder law system to qualify. Finally, there are those who have too much money to ever qualify for Medicaid but not enough to comfortably self-insure against the expenses of chronic health issues. It is this third group that has the most to lose against the costs of long-term care. And it is this same group of people for whom insurance options have been created in order for them to transfer the risk.

For a long period of time, traditional long-term care insurance policies were the norm. These policies essentially create a reimbursement scenario that covers "qualified" expenses provided by certified caregivers. Much like health insurance, if you have a need that falls under the policy's provisions for coverage, the expense will be reimbursed by the insurance company subject to policy provisions and limitations. History has shown us these policies can be problematic for two main reasons:

→ **Rate increases:** Some insurance companies historically have mispriced their long-term care coverage and have been forced to raise rates and, in some cases, bail out of the market altogether. Policies that stayed in force but were subject to large premium increases placed a large number of clients in the position of having to pay the much higher premiums (as much as a 40 percent increase in one year) or cancel coverage they had already invested in and could desperately need in the future.

→ **Use it or lose it:** Many traditional long-term care policies have no provisions for "nonforfeiture," which means if the policy owner should die without having a need to use the coverage, they simply would have spent the money on the coverage without receiving a tangible financial benefit.

Recently, the insurance industry has gotten creative in responding to the need for long-term care coverage in ways that are different from the traditional policy offerings. One of these creative solutions is a hybrid long-term care policy. Hybrid policies essentially combine the benefits of either a life insurance policy or an annuity with the benefits of long-term care coverage. While the policies can cover the same types of expenses, they are usually used as supplemental coverage to traditional payment options. In the case of the life insurance hybrid option, a rider is purchased for an extra cost on a traditional guaranteed universal life policy. The face amount of the life insurance actually serves two purposes. Obviously, it can be paid to beneficiaries in the event of the insured's death, but it can also be accessed *prior to death* to offset chronic care expenses. While these policies are not a cure-all, they do offer alternatives to the issues that have plagued traditional long-term care policies in years past.

If your head isn't spinning from all that, you're one of the few! That's why we would suggest that you consult with an expert in the area of long-term care coverage. Much like retirement income, you want to rely on experience and an analytical process to be sure you are covered as adequately as possible. Having a plan for addressing a chronic healthcare event only makes sense, and your plan should be done in the context of your overall financial resources and ability to qualify for various types of care.

What is not acceptable is to act like it won't happen to you or tell yourself that maybe the situation "will just work itself out." It is heartbreaking and devastating to see people realize they need some type of coverage after it's too late. Discovering you have a chronic health problem is not the time for this topic to become urgent. You simply won't qualify for coverage. The time to address this is when you *don't think you need it.* At the time, you may be correct, but the odds are high that there will come a day when you will. The question is, will you be prepared?

Healthcare planning for retirees is an integral part of being prepared for retirement. We realize focusing on your healthcare needs isn't as fun as planning that trip you have always wanted to go on, but it is critical that you prepare yourself for what lies ahead. Familiarize yourself with the healthcare options that exist—such as Medicare, Medicare Supplement, Medicaid, and long-term care insurance—and be sure your financial plan is **more prepared**.

→ **Don't fall for the "it won't happen to me" line of thinking.** If you could go back in time and ask, you would find that many of the people who found themselves unable to take care of themselves never thought that they would be in that situation. We all think we are bulletproof when it comes to our health and our abilities. That all changes when life deals us a set of cards that leads us to a disability, causes us to be bedridden, or clouds our mind with the insidious diseases of dementia and Alzheimer's.

→ **Don't count on Medicare or Medicaid.** The benefits for chronic healthcare needs from Medicare are very limited. Qualifying for Medicaid is next to impossible while you still have almost anything in your retirement accounts. The misguided idea of transferring those assets to other family members presents its own set of problems. In the case of IRAs or 401(k) money, you would have to pay the taxes due on the total value of the account, which means you are, in effect, giving a portion of your account to the government instead of using it for your own needs.

→ **Long-term care insurance isn't for you; *it's for your spouse and your family.*** The whole point of insuring yourself against long-term care expenses is to protect the assets (retirement accounts) you will leave to your spouse and thereafter, your children. The purchase of long-term care coverage is not an act that predetermines a care scenario for you as much as it is a move to protect the legacy you will leave to your family.

CHAPTER 6

YOUR RETIREMENT SHOULD BE **MORE PURPOS**

FUL

When you envision retirement for yourself, what pictures come to mind? Often when we speak with clients about their plans for retirement, we ask them, "What are you going to do?" Many times, they respond by telling us about their hobbies, travel plans, and indulgences they have deferred during their working years. For some, they see their retirement as an opportunity to pursue activities they enjoy more fully. Many people think about retirement as freedom, meaning that you get the paycheck, but you don't have to work to get it. That's great! But what does that actually mean? Here's a secret we can share with you that we have learned from watching people retire for many years: there are only so many golf games you can play and only so many trips you can afford. That's why we remind our clients that life after retirement has to have **purpose**, just like your life before you quit working.

You can't just retire **from** something. You should retire **to** something!

We will always remember a fellow named Troy who became

our client shortly before he left his job as an engineer with a phone company. With exhaustion in his voice, he regularly told us how he couldn't wait for retirement. His job was pressure-filled, and the rapid change in his industry was quickly causing him to struggle just to keep up. Plus, Troy said it was difficult for him to go into the office every day because the attitudes of his coworkers were negative and draining to him. Clearly, Troy was ready to retire *from* something. When we asked what he was going to do during his retirement, he told us, "Our garden has enough stuff stacked up to keep me busy for years." We helped Troy get his plan together to retire with enough income so he could comfortably replace the salary he was earning. About six months later, Troy called our office. When John answered his call, he could tell he was on a cell phone, and it sounded like he was driving a large truck. "Hey," Troy said, "I'm going to need you to cut back on the amount of money you're sending me." When John asked why, Troy said, "I've got a job driving a truck for one of my buddies! I was about to go crazy sitting around the house!" Troy didn't need the job from a financial standpoint. In fact, he was asking that we reduce his withdrawals from his retirement account. What he needed was to feel like he was fulfilling a purpose.

So, what will *your* purpose be after you clock out that last time?

It could be as simple as being the best grandparent you can be to your grandkids. It could be volunteering in your community, or you could be looking to operate on a bigger stage, so to speak. More than a decade ago, we were talking with a client about his retirement, which seemed like a long way out. We asked him our typical questions about what his retirement would look like. His answer was remarkably clear, full of purpose and passion. He said he wanted to go on mission trips to Ukraine to work with an orphanage over there and take other men in their fifties along with him. He had been several times and found great joy in serving there. He admitted others might not develop the *same* passion for that mission in going with him, but he wanted them to understand that God had a purpose for them and to show them what it looked like when you were fulfilling that purpose, as he was. He regarded his purpose as helping others find their own purpose. Now, *there's purpose!*

Throughout our book, we have highlighted topics we felt would greatly impact your success in retirement. This chapter is no different. Much the same as choosing the right advisor and having a clear plan for your financial future sets you on a path for success, having a plan for your emotional and physical well-being is critical for a successful retirement.

So, what happens when you don't have to go to work anymore? What we have observed in some retirees is a potentially dangerous set of circumstances that can spell disaster in retirement. For some, their career has defined them for the greater part of their lives and walking away from it creates a void that can lead to depression. Psychologically, when you unplug from what might well have been a very mentally active lifestyle, it's a little bit like being cast into solitary confinement. Physically, if you've been working for decades, and you suddenly stop and just watch TV, it does not do good things to your body. This drastic change in activity level can lead to major health concerns. Add to that the idea that you may suddenly find yourself living full-time with someone you may not know too well anymore while simultaneously losing strong work friendships you have developed, and the sense of physical and emotional isolation can be devastating. Therefore, our advice is to avoid being ambushed by this confluence of circumstances at all costs. Frankly, we think it might be better to continue to work than to walk into a life of undefined nothingness.

"Where there is no vision, the people perish."

—Proverbs 29:18

You probably thought the scariest part of this book would be about money, but it's not; it's about this. All the most fantastic financial advice in the world will be for naught if your retirement ends up being aimless, miserable, and short. We have shared how people avoid thinking rationally about how they will make sure they have income in the latter part of their lives. Many give even less thought to how they will prepare themselves for the social, emotional, and physical changes they will face in retirement.

The good news is that you don't have to be blindsided by these concerns. You can plan for them just like you plan for your financial needs in retirement. First, the key to being prepared is understanding your personal values. We're talking about what you value (your passions) and what you contribute to the world. It can vary greatly. Maybe world missions are in your future, like our client who planned to work in Ukraine, or maybe your contribution is going to be within your community or family. In retirement, there's a completely new opportunity to add unique value to your community and the world. And frankly, there's a physical benefit to a lot of these things. Just getting out of the house can do you a world of good. Sometimes, these opportunities present themselves in unusual ways.

One of our clients used to drive through his neighborhood, getting mad about the trash people had left lying around. It got to the point that every time he noticed it, it would infuriate him. *They* didn't pick up their trash. *They* didn't respect their own community and environment. *They* should do something about it. *They* shouldn't litter. One day, his wife came home with one of those grabber tools you can use to pick up things. Ironically, she didn't even know he was frustrated; it was just that they were getting older, and she thought that they needed help picking stuff up. But he took it as a sign and decided to go and pick up that neighborhood trash himself. This service has become part of his purpose. He values what he is doing, and he creates value in the community because it makes a difference to the people in the neighborhood to see this guy picking up trash and expecting nothing in return.

The son of a friend of ours told us a story the other day about his late father that highlights the same point. In his working life, the father was very active; he was the head of a union, a business owner, and active in the community. One day after retirement, his son drove to his dad's house and saw his dad had a pickup truck with a trailer on the back upon which was a brand-new riding lawnmower. He thought his dad was just enjoying himself with a new toy that made his life easier, but then he started seeing his dad around town, all over the place, mowing other people's yards. Assuming his father was doing this for money, the son was bothered by it. Eventually, one morning he cornered him and said, "Dad, you have plenty of money. Why are you doing this?" His dad said, "Because it needs to be done! It's what I'm supposed to do!" He had found his passion and felt his value in doing it. He was a very skilled, intelligent, accomplished man, and yet he found great satisfaction in this service: something he would never have had the time to do while he was busy pursuing his career.

Now, of course, this does have a connection to financial planning. What you plan to do with your days and weeks and months really makes a big difference to your retirement planning. Someone who's flying frequently to Ukraine will need a lot more income than someone who's going to stay local. That's why understanding this aspect of retirement is critical for us to establish what income a client is going to need during retirement. Some people retire very comfortably on $3,000 a month, and some people need $10,000 a month. Obviously, lifestyle is part of that, but also a very large part of it is what they're actually going to be *doing* in their retirement. It's very important to think about purpose in advance.

Therefore, as we've already said, one of the most important questions we ask our clients is about what comes next. We recommend brainstorming as much as you can about what your life is going to look like in retirement—well before you get there. And we're willing to bet that at some point, back years ago, you were a different person and that different person probably set aside some passions for the sake of expediency or necessity. Maybe you really loved to do certain things, but you had to go to work using a totally different set of skills to pay the bills. Well, now you have the chance to pursue your passion again. Retirement can be a whole new realm for you, but we

As Yogi Berra once said...

think you first need to go find that different person, the former you. Remember what really engaged you and then pursue that purpose with passion now that you can.

Also, understand that the nature of retirement is rapidly changing. Yogi Berra once quipped, "The future ain't what it used to be." We would definitely agree with that assessment with regard to retirement. A few years ago, we noticed a trend with people who were retiring in a new way and created a new term to describe it: *work-tirement*. We were intrigued by this new phenomenon that had people leaving the career where they had spent a significant part of their lives to take another job in a totally unrelated field. Often, money was not the issue at all. It was *purpose*. This trend of *work-tirement*, this mixing of work and retirement, is predicted to accelerate and expand. Here are a few reasons:

→ *We are living longer.* Futurists are forecasting the generation in grade school today will easily live to be 100. Advances in healthcare have already extended life expectancy in America significantly. Just think what will happen when we eventually find cures for some of the most common causes of death.

→ *Work isn't as hard as it used to be.* I know you would seriously argue this point right after a long week at your job, but the truth is that most of the work in this country has moved from physical labor to *brain work* that, while still tiring, is not as taxing on the body as manual labor. As a result of this trend, people are able to continue working long after the classic retirement age.

→ *We are resisting the notion that advancing age means declining usefulness.* Maybe it's the baby boomer's last great act of defiance, but many of us are refusing to get out of the way when it comes to work, much to the chagrin of the younger generations looking for jobs.

All this is leading to the thought that retirement will evolve into a cyclical lifestyle of work, sabbatical, re-education, and then return to work potentially within a completely different field. We call it the *wash, rinse, and repeat* lifestyle. The change likely is, in fact, being driven by necessity because of extended life expectancy and the financial strain it would place on a person to live from age 65 to 120 without a job. It's definitely something to think about.

Does this *work-tirement* trend mean retirement planning, saving, and investing will become obsolete? Not at all. You will still need income to take a break from your work and to re-educate yourself. You will need to pay your living expenses while you are reinventing yourself. And, with the evolution of this *gig economy*, in which work is seen as transient in nature, you will always need a backstop to ensure that you have a regular, predictable, dependable stream of income.

Think about when you left high school or college. If you were lucky, you were encouraged to dream big and let your imagination roam around all the possibilities that now lay before you. Where might you live? How high up the corporate ladder could you go? Maybe you'd run your own business or run for public office. Even in junior job interviews, you're often asked, "Where do you see yourself in five years?" However, as you get older, nobody asks you those questions anymore. Visionary thinking is seen as the domain of the young, so for most retirees, that muscle hasn't been exercised in a long time. That's why we encourage our clients to dream big, think big, and dare to remember what engaged their passions years ago.

Simply put, people who value what they do and add value to the world live longer, happier lives. With that in mind, take a few moments and envision your retirement filled with the activities that enrich you and the people in your life. What passions would you pursue that have been placed on hold? What opportunities exist for you to invest in the next generation or your community? Once you have finished your vision casting, share those plans and hopes with your financial advisor to ensure that your unique retirement plan provides the income you will need to realize those dreams. Retirement should be more than just passing time, and we believe retirees are uniquely positioned to passionately pursue their purpose. When we harness *the Power of MORE*, we retire to a life with *purpose and value*!

→ **Well before you retire, ask yourself: "If time and money were not an issue, what would I do?"** This line of thinking might be challenging because you will be trying to rekindle dreams you may have put away long ago in deference to the pressures of making a living. Sit down with your spouse and dream together. Don't be afraid to think outside the box and discover what your heart would have you do.

→ **While rekindling your spirit, remember your body and mind.** *Doing* requires being physically and mentally sound. Advancing age presents a challenge in both of these areas, and it takes constant effort to stave off the effects of aging. You should be intentional in this area;

you could enroll at a gym or athletic club or perhaps enjoy something less formal like a regularly scheduled walk or jog with your spouse. Staying engaged mentally through reading or writing can also allow you to add longevity to the activities you enjoy.

→ **Consider investing in others.** It has been our experience that there are very few things more gratifying to us than when we spend our time being a blessing to other people. Think about whom you might pour a portion of your life into as you begin to have the time to do so. We believe it's the key to fulfillment!

CHAPTER 7

YOUR RETIREMENT SHOULD BE MORE CONFID

ENT

At some point in retirement, it is likely that one spouse will die before the other. The husband often passes away first, and if he's typically the one who has taken care of financial matters, it can be a disaster for the surviving wife. The mourning process becomes even more overwhelming if the surviving spouse doesn't know how to manage the finances or is left without the resources necessary to function. How do you prepare *now* so that tragedy isn't compounded by financial worry later?

Janet serves a lot of widows simply because they often express a desire to have a female advisor at this stage of life. It's interesting to note that a significant number of people change their financial advisor after the death of a spouse. There are many reasons for this, but the most common is that the person left behind is not the one who was dealing with the finances before and wants to choose their own advisor as part of the process of taking charge.

Of course, it varies greatly from one family to another, but typically one person handles most of the finances and knows everything about financial arrangements, including pensions and retirement plans, and the other spouse knows very little. That means it is not uncommon for us to have a client who is, at least in the beginning, essentially clueless about what's going on with their finances and overwhelmed by the need to learn *everything all at once.*

The couple may have already been retired for some time, and everything's been fine. Now the surviving spouse has lost the smaller of the two Social Security checks and, possibly, the pension income they relied on previously. Because there is little to no financial education offered in school, the surviving spouse may not have ever paid a bill or even balanced a checkbook. Suddenly, they have to learn enough about financial matters to manage the finances alone. Especially when the death was unexpected, the spouse left behind is confronted with a sickening lack of information and is left fumbling in the darkness, frustrated, and sometimes even angry they can't ask the deceased spouse a question. On top of burying and mourning their companion of decades, they are faced with alarming questions such as, "Do I have enough income to get by? How much do I even need? Am I going to have to go back to work?" To say it's a frightening experience is an understatement. For many, it can be utterly terrifying.

Our job is to get this surviving spouse to a point at which they have at least a comfortable level of understanding. Janet grew up living and working on her family's farm, which by necessity equipped her with some very practical skills. Years ago, you needed to understand the mechanical and electrical workings of the vehicles you used because you were expected to be able to repair them when they weren't working. People who grew up that way, like Janet did, find it hard to get used to the idea that if she raises the hood on a vehicle now, like most of us, she won't understand 95 percent of what's going on under there. But she *can* drive it where she wants to go, get the oil changed, fill it up, and take care of her tires. Nowadays, beyond that, it doesn't matter. We're not terrified to use our vehicles just because we don't fully comprehend how the computer system interacts with the internal combustion engine; someone else does all that for us, and we just need a functional level of understanding of how to operate the vehicle. That same comfortable level of understanding is where we want people to be with their finances. This is never more the case than with widows or widowers.

"We're not terrified to use our vehicles just because we don't fully comprehend how the computer system interacts with the internal combustion engine..."

Often, we've found we have to do a lot of hand-holding for the first year after the death of a spouse, and then something almost magical happens. When they get past the anniversary of their loved one's death and realize they've managed to live without them for a whole year, they know they can handle it. But in that first year, there is a huge amount to learn and understand, and we tend to have a significant number of meetings. On the whole, we encourage them to make decisions when they feel able. Sometimes, however, these decisions can be urgent, especially when they're related to having enough income to continue meeting their monthly financial needs. While making allowances for the grief, we advise them to prioritize urgent matters while avoiding other decisions in the fog of grief and confusion.

Some people are totally paralyzed and completely incapable of making those decisions at first. In those cases, we recommend bringing in an adult son or daughter, or a friend who has already lost a partner. Investors in this state need someone who is there just for them and who can help them through the process. Many times, a widow doubts. "I wonder if this is what he would want me to do?" she says. There are inevitably some decisions you didn't specifically discuss, and that's OK. Your spouse would want the best for you, ultimately, regardless of the details that get you there. You have to be able to move forward without second-guessing what your deceased spouse would want.

Again, we come back to the importance of having a written plan. We always emphasize it anyway, but in this situation, it is absolutely crucial for the remaining spouse to have a written plan to which they can turn. Widows and widowers are probably not thinking clearly, and they tell us more frequently than other investors, many times after the smoke has cleared, how important it was to have a written plan. You can only take in so much in a single meeting under the best of circumstances, and it's bound to be worse if you've just lost your greatest companion and life partner. With a written plan in hand, if you wake up at two o'clock in the morning, fretting about your future financial situation, you can go through that plan and have a better understanding of where you stand, then return to bed, knowing you're OK. Of course, the best scenario is that you have a written plan that both spouses reviewed together before the situation arises.

So, what happens when the inevitable occurs, and someone is left alone? Oftentimes, priorities for investments, including income amounts, change at that point because you simply aren't supporting more than one person anymore. What comes into focus more clearly typically is the legacy the surviving person might want to leave for the children and grandchildren.

There's obviously a lot that has to change in terms of your overall income plan. At the very least, the smaller of the two Social Security checks will go away. That is important, especially if the household budget was previously based on required income at the higher level. The same concept holds true for pension income. If one of you has a pension that will either disappear or significantly decrease upon your death, you need to decide early on how you will make arrangements to replace that income. A life insurance policy might fill the gap, but there are other options too. It's all about income. A lot of people say they're going to be fine without that Social Security check because they will no longer have the expenses associated with that person. However, your expenses don't get cut in half when one spouse dies. Sure, the grocery bill does, but living expenses such as the mortgage, taxes, utilities, and car payments do not.

Without being gloomy, we feel compelled to tell you that it's a mistake to think this scenario is only likely to happen later in life. We have widows in their thirties with young children who thought their husbands were healthy, until one day they didn't come home. This can happen at any time. It's important for both partners to have a comfortable understanding of their finances at all stages of life. We want the surviving family members to be able to maintain their current standard of living.

With regard to putting life insurance in place ahead of time, we thoroughly recommend it. We've seen the full range of outcomes from decisions about life insurance. We have helped families who used it to put adequate finances in place, thereby leaving the surviving spouse and children able to maintain their lifestyle. Sadly, we have also helped clients for whom this provision was not made, with disastrous consequences. True, if you have a widow with young children, they're going to receive Social Security benefits, but there is a cap on those as well as a cap on what the widow can earn while receiving those benefits. We can assure you it's an insanely low number, and, if you are dependent on those benefits, you're likely not going to be able to maintain the standard of living you previously had.

Life insurance is one of the best ways to address this issue, and, frankly, the cost doesn't have to be prohibitive. When we look at life insurance, we always ask, "If one of you didn't live past tomorrow, how much income would the other spouse need?" The answer to that question helps you determine the level of life insurance you need. Fifty thousand dollars in coverage isn't going to replace your spouse's annual income or even most of it. You'll be able to bury them with that and have a small amount left to cover other expenses, but you may need to replace all or most of your spouse's current and future unearned income. Keep in mind life insurance doesn't really insure your life at all. It should be called "income replacement insurance," as that is its true purpose.

Going back to the imbalanced spouse situation regarding

financial knowledge, it's incredibly important to avoid the scenario where one spouse simply zones out whenever it comes to making decisions about money. We see this scenario happening more often than we're comfortable with. Many people are tempted to hand over responsibility to the other spouse. We often hear, "They're better at it than I am," or "I don't understand this," or "That's their thing." But at some point, it will be *your* thing, and you are going to have to understand it! It's better to learn together now than alone when it's urgent.

While you're working on other areas together, you should also deal with an estate plan. A lot of people assume that because they have a will, their estate won't go to probate, but this is simply not true. We see huge advantages in getting a solid estate plan together while both spouses are still living. Also, after the death of a spouse, it should be on the survivor's checklist to update the estate plan. It's not an immediate, urgent task, but it should be done. A widow or widower will most likely want to change the beneficiaries on all the accounts they now control. One of our clients is a 60-year-old widower who is still working. We changed everything we were responsible for here, but we also took the time to ask if he'd changed the beneficiary on his 401(k) plan. He had a lost look on his face as he replied that he didn't know. It's important to keep a list of things you need to address, such as beneficiary changes, and to check those off as they're completed. Typically, updating beneficiary information involves naming children as beneficiaries, possibly in trust if they're not yet old enough to handle an inheritance or if the estate-planning attorney recommends this approach for other reasons. This is one of the many issues that should be addressed in preparing your revised estate plan.

Is it a good idea to get a lawyer, too? Yes, but preferably before the first spouse dies. *Be cautious* about the person from whom you're seeking legal advice. If your brother is your primary care physician, and you have a heart problem, you go to see a cardiologist, not your brother. By the same token, a regular attorney might not necessarily be the right choice; you likely need someone who specializes in estate planning, just as you would seek the specialization of a cardiologist.

Working with a recently bereaved spouse, many of the questions we ask and issues we raise go far beyond the realm of investments. We've stepped in, helped, and advised on an almost unimaginable range of matters over the years. We recently helped a widow extricate herself from a terrible lease arrangement on a vehicle and get more affordable transportation. While that doesn't normally come under the heading of duties of a financial advisor, it was simply the right thing to do. She needed help and still couldn't think straight. We had a contact who could help her, and she was incredibly grateful for it. Sometimes you simply need somebody to hold your hand for a while through the journey.

One thing you can do together right now is create a *Honey, I Love You* file, so that, if one of you doesn't come home one day, everything the other person needs is in this file. It should include a listing of all insurance policies and the pertinent information that goes along with them. It should say where you can locate birth certificates, marriage certificates, passports, Social Security cards, etc. There should also be information in there, if it applies, about military service. That's very important to be able to locate quickly; a lot of people don't know that the funeral or burial costs of someone who served can be covered, a benefit that is important for the surviving spouse to understand. Obviously, the file should include information about all retirement accounts, with the written plan in there too!

We have a significant concern that the more digital we become, the more inundated people become with junk in their e-mail accounts. You can sign up to receive everything electronically, but beware! In generations past, you might not have known that grandpa had a $50,000 CD at the bank, but when the snail mail came, you'd know. What do you do if all the statements are electronic, and you don't have access to your spouse's e-mail? We predict that there will be increasing millions of dollars that go unclaimed because survivors don't know how to access accounts or don't even know that they exist at all. So, make sure all your accounts and passwords are in there, too, or think about signing up for a password management program on your computer and phone so that your spouse only needs one password to access everything.

Generally, if you have adult children whom you trust, it's a really good idea to bring them into the planning process while everybody is cognitively strong. There truly is a lot to be said for involving your children in estate and retirement planning all around. In our experience, it's often a huge help to have an adult child around when the situation is laid out clearly to a now-single parent. The child can help make decisions, some of which have to be made early on, purely for practical, cash-flow purposes, while the grieving process is still at its peak. We believe it's incredibly beneficial to include in that process those children who already have an understanding of their parents' needs and wants. It's a whole different thing to be grieving the loss of a parent rather than grieving the loss of a lifelong spouse. Additionally, the companionship is extremely important.

As one of Janet's pastors jokingly says, "None of us is getting out of here alive. I've checked the statistics on it, and I'm pretty sure I'm right." The UK's *Guardian* newspaper reported recently that some 800,000 women in the United States will lose their spouses this year. We pray you are not among them, but we also pray you take the time to make sure you are prepared. A written plan and the proper safeguards will ensure that you or your loved ones are able to handle whatever lies ahead in your absence. So, with all that a surviving spouse will need to face, do you believe that both of you are prepared to confidently take the reins of your finances when the time comes?

→ **For married couples, the chance of one spouse living for years following the death of the other is about 80 percent.** There have been well-documented cases of what's known as the "widowhood effect." Johnny and June Cash died within four months of one another, and the parents of former NFL quarterback Doug Flutie died just an hour apart. But in most cases, life goes on for one of you, often for years. If you don't know much about your money, take the time to get up to speed. You don't have to replace the financial leader right now; you just have to be ready should the responsibility become yours.

→ **It's a family affair.** Talking about money with your spouse and your adult children can be uncomfortable. Just the thought of considering your own demise can cause even the most confident personalities to shrink from the conversation. From assisting you with financial matters after your spouse's death to the details of the orderly transfer of your estate, family or very close friends need to be involved.

→ **Bring an attorney into the discussion to be sure everything is done right.** Where we live, it's common to see people set up what we have called "country folks estate planning," which basically involves making the adult children joint owners on real estate and financial assets. Such a strategy is fraught with problems and should be avoided. Instead, an estate-planning attorney can be helpful in making sure things pass in an orderly fashion from spouse to spouse, and then from parent to children. Be sure to discuss your "digital estate," which are your online accounts.

CHAPTER 8

YOUR RETIREMENT SHOULD BE **MORE WISE**

"Can't you see this is the Land of Confusion?"

—*Genesis, 1986*

As we have pointed out, we live in a world where we are drowning in information, yet we are starved for knowledge. To take it a step further, what we really need is wisdom when it comes to making decisions about our retirement. You might ask if knowledge and wisdom are not the same. They aren't. Knowledge is the accumulation of information through education. Wisdom is the *soundness* of an action or decision with regard to the *application* of knowledge and good judgment. Wisdom is often acquired when information and experience intersect.

When it comes to retirement and the financial complexities of trying to live the rest of your life without a job and a paycheck, how do you acquire wisdom? After all, it's not like you get a practice run or experience retirement more than once.

Let's address where you might get some help. The media is loaded with financial "gurus" who profess lots of knowledge about

"As we have pointed out, we live in a world where we are drowning in information, yet we are starving for knowledge."

money and finances. But think about it: none of those gurus know absolutely anything about you and your situation. Earlier, we said that your retirement should be "more personal." You certainly won't get that from the folks who only write or talk about personal finance but **never engage in the practice of the profession**. What you will get from the gurus are a lot of broad statements that can do more harm than good. Here are a few examples:

➔ "*Everyone* should have gold in their portfolios."

➔ "No one should *ever* own an annuity."

➔ "You should *never* use a credit card."

➔ "You should *never* buy permanent life insurance."

Gurus love to use these blanket statements as part of their "advice" they offer to the listening and viewing public. Their comments should be a warning sign.

Our experience tells us there are very few generalizations that hold up to scrutiny when confronted with real-life financial issues and problems. These people have created a pop culture with such generalizations because they appeal to the human need and desire to go along with the crowd. "Everyone is putting their money in _____." Or, "No one should ever do_____." Such a herd mentality is neither helpful nor accurate. In fact, we will say this: there is **never** a generalization that applies to everyone's financial situation. (Wait—did we just do that?)

Here is the problem with these pop culture mavens. They make these overly broad pronouncements with the fervor of a Pentecostal preacher, convincing the masses that certain financial products have the qualities of the devil. In their audience is someone who may, in fact, need the very product they have just berated. When that person goes to seek financial advice from an actual practitioner, they cannot be convinced of their need for said product because the guru said it was evil and that they should never use it! By listening to a guru, that person may never get their problem solved in a proper way.

Full disclosure: we do a radio show in which we discuss financial issues that airs across the state of Arkansas every week. However, in the opening moments of every show, we have an announcer who says: "Relying on someone who doesn't know you or your situation to give you specific financial advice is just plain dumb. That's why everything said on this show is just helpful information. If you want specifics, give us a call." And that's the way it should be. Remember, prescription without diagnosis is malpractice.

Many years ago, John had the somewhat harrowing experience of discovering his taxi driver on a business trip was slightly inebriated. There are some priceless moments about that cab ride that we won't go into, but the most memorable thing was the answer to virtually every question John asked the driver on the trip: "Been there, done that!" And while we don't recommend trying to duplicate John's travel experience, it would be to your advantage to find a retirement advisor who has "Been there, done that!" It is in that relationship where wisdom can be shared, and you can be the beneficiary of that wisdom.

In seeking out someone to partner with, you will be faced with a lot of people who want to give you retirement advice. Only a few are likely to be fully qualified and experienced enough to navigate the complexities of your situation. One of the first things you need to know is the background of the advisor. Fortunately, the résumé and regulatory history of advisors are available at brokercheck.finra.org and adviserinfo.sec.gov. If someone is not registered on either of these databases, they are not registered investment advisors or registered representatives of any securities firm. Absent these registrations, someone is likely either not qualified to provide the type of advice you need (e.g., insurance agents selling financial products), or they may be someone posing as an advisor with bad intentions. **Keep in mind, simply being registered with no negative history does not qualify someone to be your retirement advisor, but it does get them past the first major test.**

Secondly, you need to know: *How many clients have you/ your firm actually helped to retire?* While volume is not the lone indicator, an advisor obviously has got to be *in the game* in order to have the experience. So, having a successful track record would be a prerequisite.

Next, we would ask: *How many of your clients are like me?* It's important that your advisor is used to working with the type of client you will be. If you are constrained in the amount of money you have available for retirement, you have a different set of challenges ahead of you than the person who has a multimillion-dollar portfolio. Be sure your advisor has the experience to help you with your unique circumstances.

Once you are in front of an advisor and engaging in a discussion about your retirement, ask *yourself* an important question: *Do I understand what they are saying?* If one of our advisors were to walk into your place of business, it's likely they would understand little of what you do, especially if you used the jargon of your industry. The same thing applies when it comes to retirement planning. Our profession is not something you do every day, and just because you made the money and saved it doesn't mean you have to be an expert at managing it. However, it is important that you have a base-level knowledge of the strategies, products, and objectives of the work of your advisor. In our practice, we have adopted a *10 to 2* mandate, which in short means taking the complex information (level 10) and making it simple to understand (level 2).

Next question: ***Will you provide me with a written, comprehensive plan for my retirement?*** Remember that startling statistic from chapter 1? Only 16 percent of near-term retirees have a written retirement income plan. Don't be a statistic. Your advisor may very well charge you for writing such a plan—and it will likely be worth every penny. The plan will be the roadmap for your finances as you begin your journey into the next phase of life. It will serve as your foundation when things get crazy in the market, when some unexpected life event crops up, and, yes, even when your memory fades as you advance in age. In our practice, we employ the *GenWealth Ready-to-Retire Process* as the framework upon which we build a client's retirement income plan. Remember, *a written plan is essential.*

You should also ask: ***Will you be my only advisor, or will other*** *people be involved in working with me?* This question is important for several reasons. Your financial future should not be dependent on the advice or the availability of one person. Advisors take vacations, travel to training conferences, have babies, get sick, and sometimes just need a day off. That shouldn't mean you should have to wait until they get back to have your needs met. Your lead advisor should have a depth of talent around them to help you when they are unavailable. Those team members should also be qualified to step up should the advisor retire, become disabled, or die. It is important to know what happens to you if something happens to them.

This next question is often on the minds of clients, but some people are intimidated to broach the subject: *How are you compensated?* The point of this question is not to use an advisor who is compensated one way or the other. It is for you to understand that all investments have some type of cost involved and to understand what is in it for your advisor. As a matter of fact, you should want your advisor to be well compensated. They are running a business whose purpose is to serve you for years to come. They must make a profit in order to be able to do that in the future.

Advisors may charge a financial planning fee for providing you the written document outlining the strategy for your retirement income. At that point, you are free to implement that plan anywhere, including with the advisor who designed the plan. In most cases, that is the most effective method. Implementation means acquiring the investments and products necessary to make the plan work.

Many advisors are what our profession calls "dually registered." That simply means the advisor is able to charge either fees or commissions. Despite a lot of noise in the press, there is no inherent flaw in either method of compensation. Fees are appropriate for actively managed accounts, compensating the advisor for his or her work in selecting investments, reallocating your portfolio, updating your plan and so forth. Commissions may be appropriate for investments that you will purchase and hold for a long period of time, that don't require active, discretionary management on the part of your advisor.

It is common to hear that advisors are overly incentivized to sell high-commission products. However, the Department of Labor Fiduciary Rule has had the effect of leveling commissions on categories of investment products and requiring advisors to act in the client's best interest when dealing with their retirement accounts. Note that, at the time of this writing, the rule is on hold yet again; however, many of the intentions of the rule, including leveled compensation, have already been adopted by many broker-dealers across the country.

One final note on this subject: there is an element to the relationship that sits squarely on your shoulders. It's the element of discernment. Are you satisfied that the advisor truly has your best interest at the forefront of your relationship? Does the advisor ask a lot of questions about you and your financial situation or do they talk a lot about products? There is a time to have that product focus, but it should only come after they understand your needs. Does the staff of the office appear to be professional and capable of serving your interests now and into the future? Your perceptions are equally as important as the answers to the questions we have offered you.

Earlier, we mentioned that finding an advisor with the heart of a teacher is a critical step in your journey. For wisdom to be impactful in your retirement income plan, it must be effectively imparted. We believe that finding an advisor who will not only put together a great plan, but will also take the time to make sure you understand the plan, will help you harness the *Power of MORE* in your retirement.

→ **No do-overs.** Retirement income planning is one of those things you don't get a second chance to get right. We believe that finding the right team to work with in planning, executing, and maintaining your plan is critical. Carefully evaluate the history, training, strategy, and compatibility of those you are thinking about working with. You should stay away from anyone who doesn't have a well-structured system for supporting a lifelong client relationship.

→ **Decide to share the cockpit.** Like the pilot in command of an airliner, you are in charge of your money and your retirement. We don't advocate taking a passive role in your relationship with an advisor;

rather, we believe that the advisor should be your copilot, sharing responsibilities for the journey. Your advisor has areas of expertise. Rely on them and let them do their job. Your job is to evaluate the direction and the outcomes the advisor is designing. Working together, it can be a smooth flight.

➔ **Embrace the process.** Take the list of questions in this chapter and engage with an advisor who fits the characteristics we've outlined. The relationship with an advisory firm should be a two-way street with open communication, trust, and mutual benefit. If you aren't comfortable with the things you hear in the conversation, keep looking.

EPILOGUE

ARE YOU READY FOR **MORE?**

Now it's your turn. We have laid out a vision of how harnessing the *Power of MORE* in your retirement can potentially change the destiny of your next phase of life. You have to add the essential ingredient to make all this a reality: ACTION.

After years of meeting with families looking to retire, one thing is very clear to us. You've got to be a participant rather than a spectator. Faced with a torrent of information, many people seize up with *analysis paralysis.* Don't do it. Here are the broad strokes of what you need to know.

In an industry that is so prone to cookie-cutter advice, we believe your retirement should be more personal with a plan that is specifically crafted for your particular circumstances. Your retirement is not the time for a fumble in the proverbial red zone. You don't have time for a do-over or a mulligan. Your plan has to be about you, and it has to create the outcome you are seeking.

In this era of disappearing pensions and a questionable future for Social Security, dependability of income should be a high priority for you as you seek to find the right path in creating predictable income for the rest of your life. You should make sure you don't just have an investment plan for your retirement. A strategic, comprehensive, written plan that encompasses every area of your financial life can serve you well and keep you on track. Be it the *GenWealth Ready-to-Retire Process* or some other plan, the qualities of being on paper and *on purpose* are essential.

Think about how much your life has changed since you became an adult. Retirement is what we call Life 2.0, and it, too, is full of change. Many of those changes are not pleasant—like the death of a spouse or failing health. Being MORE prepared won't change those eventualities, but it could make dealing with them easier.

Life 2.0 is much better (and in many cases longer) with a clearly defined purpose. What's yours? This time of your life is something you've never experienced before. Other than your spouse, whom will you rely upon for wisdom and guidance into this uncharted territory? Once you find your coach, listen to them and follow their advice. They have the advantage of experience, emotional detachment, and objectivity to keep you from doing the wrong thing, at the wrong time, for the wrong reason. At GenWealth Financial Advisors, we call that "being coachable."

Again, don't allow your indecision to become your decision and cause you to miss what the *Power of MORE* can do for you and your family. Whether it is with us or another financial advisor, find that relationship and get started today.

ABOUT THE AUTHORS

John Shrewsbury's start in broadcast journalism laid a foundation for his capacity to communicate complex topics like personal finance and retirement planning in a simple, understandable way. In 1996, John moved his family from his hometown of El Dorado in south Arkansas to the central part of the state to build what is now GenWealth Financial Advisors.

In 2002, when **Janet Walker** and her husband returned to their home state from Tennessee, she and John began to work together to bring education about money matters to the people of Arkansas. Janet was first a teacher and will always be an educator at heart; she uses her passion for education to teach her clients about financial independence.

After working together for a period of time, John and Janet formed GenWealth Financial Advisors in 2005 and have since grown to more than thirty advisors and administrative personnel. Joining their talents in broadcasting and teaching, John and Janet began "The Get Ready for the Future" radio show in 2007, which is now the longest-running financial talk show in the state. Each Saturday morning on stations across Arkansas, John, Janet and their team deliver "straight talk about retirement, investments and your money."

Today, John, Janet and the GenWealth team have enabled thousands of people to shift from learning about money to pursuing their goals of financial independence and transitioning from work to life.

CPSIA information can be obtained
at www.ICGtesting.com
Printed in the USA
LVHW081742041121
702297LV00006BA/9